THE LAST DAYS OF STEAM IN
OXFORDSHIRE

THE LAST DAYS OF STEAM IN
OXFORDSHIRE

– KEVIN ROBERTSON –

ALAN SUTTON
1987

ALAN SUTTON PUBLISHING
BRUNSWICK ROAD · GLOUCESTER

First published 1987

British Library Cataloguing in Publication Data

Robertson, Kevin
Last days of steam in Oxfordshire.
1. Locomotives—England—Oxfordshire—
History—Pictorial works
I. Title
625.2′61′094257   TJ603.4.G7

ISBN 0-86299-332-6
SU/135/1140–1008/R/080687/3200

*Endpapers: 'Totnes Castle' passing Bledlow's down distant signal on a
Paddington bound express, 9.9.50. – J.F. Russell Smith*

Front Cover: No. 7023, 'Penrice Castle' passing Finstock Halt on 27.7.63 – A Molyneaux

*Back Cover: Steam at rest, with sunshine and shadows penetrating the interior
of the Oxford shed – J.R. Fairman*

Typesetting and origination by
Alan Sutton Publishing Limited
Printed in Great Britain by
The Bath Press, Avon

Introduction

As a county, Oxfordshire is famous for many things. The beautiful city of Oxford, the various county palaces and of course a number of villages and smaller towns all of which have played their part in the development of the county.

To the railway enthusiast Oxfordshire in the days of steam will always be renowned for its variety of locomotives. Representatives from each of the four main line groups as well as the BR standard engines, were all regular visitors to its lines. Also, apart from the locomotives, the rail routes themselves are a fascinating story. A number of different companies were represented, although eventually all had been absorbed into one of three concerns, the Great Western, London Midland & Scottish and London & North Eastern companies.

At nationalisation in 1948 British Railways inherited a jumble of machines and routes. Main lines as well as branches and of course all the stock necessary to operate over them.

The period from 1948 to the end of steam was one of slow change and saw both the elimination of various steam locomotive classes as well as the introduction of several new ones, referred to as the BR Standard designs. Many of these new engines were to have a very brief life for steam working had all but vanished in the county by the beginning of 1966.

With such a variety of steam engines working within the county making a selection of photographs has been especially difficult. Added to which changes in the county boundaries mean some places are now in Oxfordshire that were not before and of course vice-versa. The final selection is very much a personal choice and I beg the indulgence of the reader if we creep over the border from time to time. The intention is to show not only the locomotives and trains but the other features of a now vanished railway scene. If a few memories are rekindled all will have been worthwhile.

Kevin Robertson

THE LAST DAYS OF STEAM IN
OXFORDSHIRE

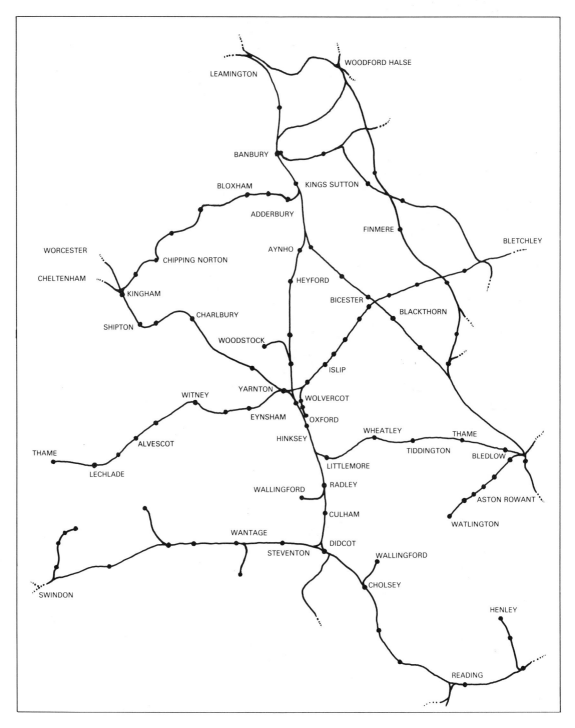

LAST DAYS OF STEAM IN OXFORDSHIRE

Only locations relevant to the text are shown

OXFORD

SEE BRITAIN BY TRAIN

In the 1950s British Railways produced a series of colour posters depicting the various locations they served. The one for Oxford was to the design of Linford and in traditional contemporary styling. The image successfully portrays the 'City of gleaming spires'.

British Railways

During the 1950s many of the stopping passenger and lesser express services were in the hands of 'Hall' class engines. 4934 *Hindlip Hall* working an up train near Appleford during the early years of BR.

Collection of P. T. Earl

As recounted in the introduction the difficulty of portraying the railways of Oxfordshire is in the changes made to the county boundaries. Although on the reverse side there is far more scope in choosing photographs. With a little bit of licence, this is Didcot during steam days and before Berkshire relinquished administrative control of the town. Who then could resist such a view to start with Didcot based 2–8–0, No. 3820 about to enter the yards at Didcot North Junction with a freight from Oxford on 9.5.1964.

Rodney Lissenden

The importance of the line through Oxford southwards was to a large extent due to its freight traffic. Countless freight trains conveyed products from the industrial midlands to the south coast ports and London markets via Reading. In addition there were the empty workings, intended to provide wagons for the various main yards after which they were distributed as required. One of these empty trains near Appleford in charge of a later series '43xx Mogul', No. 7340 in May 1964.

Rodney Lissenden

Just north of Appleford Crossing was Appleford Halt, the delightful sounding name probably taken from the numerous fruit orchards around the area. The halt dated from 1933, one of a number opened throughout the system in an effort to counter the threat from the first 'bus services. In 1959 its appearance was little altered from 26 years previously, with railway tickets still obtained from the local agent. Supporting the sign is a piece of bridge rail, probably dating from the 19th century. Today the station is still open although tickets have to be purchased from the train guard.

P. Rickard

The four track section of track from London ended at Appleford Crossing north of Didcot and was the scene on 11.9.52 of an accident when a freight train over-ran the loop and demolished the signal box. When the dust had settled, little of the 'box was left standing although the engineers were soon at work so that just four weeks later the structure was rebuilt and to almost the same style as before. The nameboard was one of the few items it was possible to salvage from the previous structure.

British Railways

An unusual appearance was that of 46251 *City of Nottingham* on a special organised by the 'Railway Correspondence & Travel Society' on 9.5.64. The big pacific was already redundant from its front line role on the main line from Euston and was only a short way from withdrawal. The train was destined eventually for Portsmouth with 46251 in charge for part of the trip only, the engine not allowed to run over Southern lines as clearances were insufficient.

Rodney Lissenden

By contrast on the same day as 46251 worked her special train there was also the usual procession of more mundane services, including this one hauled by a grimy 2–6–0, No. 6367 seen between Appleford and Culham. Such sights were taken for granted at the time but are now long vanished from the railway scene.

Rodney Lissenden

As in other areas the variety of steam engines during the 1950s and 60s was one of the main attractions to the lineside photographer. All the more so when a special working brought something even more unusual. This was the case for a short while from 1957 with *City of Truro* restored for service from the Didcot shed yet also working a number of enthusiasts specials. One of these was on 16.6.57, with a Swindon–Birmingham 'Stephenson Locomotive Society' train. 3440 in charge on the return working of the special near Appleford Crossing.

R.C. Riley

Of the three intermediate stopping places between Didcot and Oxford, undoubtably the most important was Radley, the station portraying the usual features associated with a former GWR location. Today, however, most of what can be seen on the photograph has been swept away leaving just the main lines and two platforms each with just a bus shelter type structure. Some years before this; No. 2912 *Saint Ambrose* enters the station with an 'up' or London bound stopper. The 'Saint' class engines were forerunners of the later 'Hall' class. The family similarity between the various classes of western engines is apparent from the various photographs.

R.H.G. Simpson

Disturbing the peace at Radley, 34009 *Lyme Regis* hurries through the station with the 10.00 a.m. Bradford–Poole service on 17.8.63. Southern pacifics worked several of the through inter-regional services as far as Oxford returning south with a balanced working. The numbered board hanging from the smokebox is an indication of the duty number for the crew who came from Bournemouth shed.

E. Wilmshurst

As portrayed on the station nameboard in the previous photograph Radley was also the junction for the short branch to Abingdon, more of which can be seen later. 14xx tank engine, No. 1420 waiting in the loop platform at the head of a single coach Abingdon train on 13.9.58. The main lines to and from Oxford are on the right hand side of the canopy.

A.E. Bennett

Trundling though Radley bunker first, an unidentified pannier tank heads south for Didcot. In the picture on the right is Radley signal box its position on the platform meaning passengers were able to see inside at an aspect of railway work not usually visible.

R.H.G. Simpson

At a sedate pace an unidentified 28xx 2–8–0 slowly emerges from the up loop onto the main line with a stopping freight. A train such as this would be likely to be diverted into most passing loops so as not to impede the passage of faster trains, the journey between Oxford and Reading taking two hours or more to cover the 28 miles.

R.H.G. Simpson

Just beyond Radley station the four track section began again, the up and down relief lines continuing as far as Hinksey Yard a little way south of Oxford station. Seen from the roadbridge a freight from Abingdon makes its way towards Hinksey, made up of a number of brand new MG sports cars from the factory at Abingdon.

R.H.G. Simpson

For much of its route through Oxford the railway was almost level with the surrounding land, dissected by numerous tributaries serving the River Thames. With one of these alongside the line 5061 approaches Hinksey South with a Margate–Birkenhead through train on 15.8.59.

R.C. Riley

Before reaching Hinksey was Kennington Junction and the point of divergence for the branch through Thame to Princes Risborough. A freight in charge of BR. Class 5, 73114 *Etarre* is seen just north of the junction on 25.7.62 travelling on the the up main line and with the signal set to continue south towards Didcot.

R.C. Riley

Part of the appeal of Oxford was its undoubted variety of engines on regular daily workings. The Southern 'Lord Nelson' class were regular visitors until ousted by the Bulleid Pacifics. Before this though 30861 *Lord Anson* passes the southernmost exit from Hinksey Yard with a Poole–Bradford train in 1959. To the right the bracket signal controls the exit from the yard onto the main line, the ringed arms indicating this is a goods line only.

R.C. Riley

As with goods wagons it was often necessary to move empty coaching stock around to suit operational requirements. A number of these workings took place at holiday weekends and in the summer months when the operating authorities were faced with a continual problem of insufficient stock where it was needed. Finding engines to move the stock was also a problem although here an ex-LMS 8F is being used, 48412 in charge of an up empty stock train at Hinksey South just south of Oxford in the summer of 1959.

R.C. Riley

The marshalling yards at Hinksey were brought into use in 1942, and were of considerable strategic importance to the movement of essential traffic. Their use, however, faded over the years so that coinciding with the end of steam, the yards too were closed. On 29.8.59, 5960 *Saint Edmund Hall* passes Hinksey South with a through service from Newcastle–Bournemouth. The train is made up of coaches from the Midland, Eastern and Southern regions.

E. Wilmshurst

From the same vantage point a few years earlier *Dukedog* No. 9008 is seen travelling south on the main line. Despite their antiquated appearance these engines were of relatively recent construction utilising various parts from older machines and so obtaining maximum usage from still serviceable equipment. Their last outpost, however, was some way distant on the Cambrian lines in mid-Wales, and perhaps meaning 9008 was on its way towards Swindon and withdrawal.

R.H.G. Simpson

Oxford, city of gleaming spires, with 1335 against a suitable background at Oxford shed in 1951. No. 1335 was one of three 2–4–0 members of the class taken over from the MSWJ company in 1923. For many years the engines worked in the Oxford–Didcot–Reading area on light trains and on which they were eminently suitable. Along with her sisters, however, 1335 was not to have a long life under BR being an early casualty. Had she survived a few years longer it is almost certain one of these historically important engines would have been preserved.

Collection of P. T. Earl

Another 8F but this time on the sort of duty for which they were intended. No. 48431 at the head of a long train of coal and other freight immediately south of Oxford station on Sunday 11.9.60.

M. Mensing

The London & North Western Railway together with their successors the LMS had their own station at Oxford for many years although this did not prevent LNWR designed engines from venturing onto western metals as required. 1912 'G2a' Bowen–Cooke design No. 49287 leaving the south yard at Oxford (western) with an unfitted freight on 29.9.56.

R.C. Riley

Arriving at Oxford on 30.10.65 with the northbound 'Pines Express', 34019 *Bideford* makes a cautious approach to the station. During the last years certain engines seemed to monopolise this train, 34019 and 34102 working turn and turn about for much of the period 1965/6.

Courtney Haydon

After servicing and if necessary refuelling, the Southern engine would run through the station to await its trains arrival from the north. 34019 starting back southwards for Didcot, Reading, Basingstoke and Bournemouth. Behind the tender the train is made up of BR Mark 1 coaching stock painted maroon whilst underneath the layers of grime the engine was in brunswick green livery.

Courtney Haydon

Busy times at Oxford, with four engines visible and from three different regions! In the left foreground is an LNWR 0–8–0; next to it is a Western 'Hall'. Facing the 0–8–0 is a Southern pacific whilst another 'Hall' lurks in the background alongside the south signal box. The ladder crossover allowed access to and from the Beckett Street yard on the right, the yard was also used for local coal traffic with several wagons alongside the merchants wharves

R.H.G. Simpson

By September 1966 steam was a rarity at Oxford, the few workings that remained often coming from the Southern and Midland regions. On the main line in place of steam were the diesels, D1924 one of three 'Brush' or Class 47's allocated to the southern and seen here in charge of the southbound 'Pines Express'. Alongside is *Hymek* D7061, which along with the larger 'Western' class were arguably some of the best looking diesel designs. Unfortunately the 'Hymek' class was one of those destined for early withdrawal as it possessed non-standard hydraulic transmission. None of the class are now working on BR.

D. Fereday Glenn

Another Southern visitor in the form of 34084 *253 Squadron* on its way from the shed to take over a train and with the attention of both the driver and fireman attracted by a unknown incident on the platform. Frustrating not knowing what it was!

Len Davies

A few years before the diesels and prior to the advent of the Bulleid Pacifics 'King Arthur' class engines had also been used on the inter-regional trains. 30783 *Sir Gillemere* attached to a Leicester–Southampton service on a wet 29.8.59 and awaiting the right-away.

A.E. Bennett

In the same place 6852 *Headbourne Grange* on the through road at the north end of the station. The centre lines of the station were used primarily for freight and light engine working and so avoided obstructing the two platform faces. The last years seeing few non-stop passenger trains through Oxford.

Collection of M. Sumner

Besides southern and midland engines, visitors from the Eastern Region were common, B1, 61209 just arrived with a train probably from Leicester. After uncoupling the engine will make its way to the shed after which the train will be remade ready for the return working. Eastern coaching stock rarely worked further south towards Didcot.

W. Gilburt

One of the last regular turns for the ex-LNER B12 class was on the Bletchley services, 61577 in the process of being uncoupled after arriving with the 12.10 p.m. service on 6.6.59.

Courtney Haydon

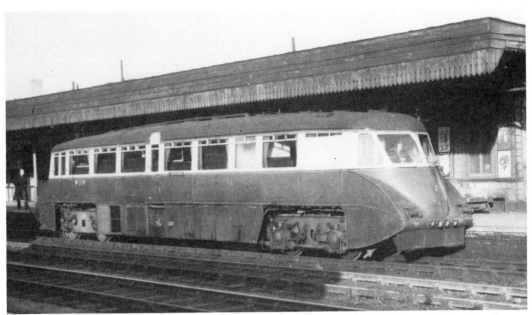

Variety again and this time one of the former GWR streamlined diesel railcars. At the time these units were introduced in the early 1930's they were the very latest in design and comfort. Whilst 20 years later the interiors were certainly very comfortable, changing fashions had resulted in a decidedly dated appearance. W2W on an Oxford–Princes Risborough stopping service, 13.11.54.

W. Gilburt

Alongside the north end of the down platform were the Cripley sidings used primarily for coaching stock storage. Here a Worcester based engine, 5071 *Spitfire* waits in the sidings with what will later form a stopping service to Wolverhampton. The use of a 'Castle' for shunting work was a far from common practice. On the extreme left is a two car diesel unit with a train for Bletchley, 11.9.60

M. Mensing

To a design dating back to 1911, 5390 trundles through Oxford northwards on a bright autumn evening, 29.9.56

R.C. Riley

By comparison with the seemingly endless procession of 'Castles' and 'Halls' a 'County' was a much rarer type. No 1009 *County of Cardigan* depicted with the early BR tender logo and attached to an SR rake of coaches, indicative then of another through working.

W. Gilburt

Oxford station itself was little more than a ramshakle wooden affair which suffered from numerous add-ons over the years. It was not until the 1970's that a complete rebuild took place, although even then in perhaps a rather untidy style. Years before university students arriving at the station would arrange with the station master to cash their cheques at the booking office, indeed as one was later to remark, ". . .what else were station masters for?"

Courtney Haydon

On their way back to the loco shed, ex-LMS 8F No. 48271 and BR standard 73003 slowly back through the station. According to local residents steam engines and Oxford did not go well together. To combat an almost continual stream of complaints, notices were posted around the area reminding crews to keep the emission of smoke to a minimum.

Courtney Haydon

Two mechanical signal boxes controlled the immediate station area. Both lasted until 1973 and the installation of MAS to Oxford. The north 'box was basically a timber structure the lower half surrounded (from 1940) by a brick shell intended to provide a degree of protection against bomb blast. Fortunately this was never put to the test.

Courtney Haydon.

Three years after the introduction of the first diesels onto the Western Region certain services remained steam hauled including many Worcester line trains. Worcester shed was also renowned for its clean engines, 7002 *Devizes Castle* a typical example just entering Oxford station with the 9.17 a.m. Great Malvern–Paddington service on 23.7.61.

P.J. Kelley

Inside the north 'box and showing part of the 100 lever frame. Two signalmen and a booking boy are on duty, the latter position a form of apprenticeship into the signalman grade. Despite its elderly appearance the stove was very efficient at warming the building. The disadvantage being that when a wire broke as the signalman was pulling a lever, it left the man sitting on top of the fire.

R.H.G. Simpson

With the LNWR engine shed just visible in the background D16 4–4–0 No. 62585 slowly backs out of the up bay platform after bringing in a train from Cambridge. 27.2.54

R.C. Riley

Alongside a maze of point rodding and signal wires 4993 *Dalton Hall* passes sister engine 4995 on the western loco shed and enters Oxford station on a Wolverhampton–Paddington train. This particular service was one of those routed via the Thame branch to Princes Risborough, travelling then through High Wycombe and Denham to London. Interestingly, the engine carries an 81D, Reading, shedplate although it is not going anywhere near its home depôt.

R.C. Riley

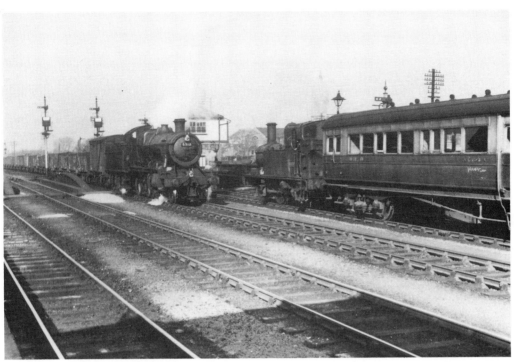

Almost neck and neck, 6313 on the up main with a through freight whilst 14xx No. 1420 arrives at the up platform with the auto-train from the Woodstock branch.

R.C. Riley

Another 'Hall' this time 4956 *Plowden Hall* and allocated at the time to Hereford leaving Oxford with the ten coach 7.10 a.m. Paddington–Wolverhampton service on 15.7.59. In the background the silhouettes of the signals stand out well, clearly showing the ideal position for signals against a sky background. Also discernable is an unidentified WD 2–8–0 probably waiting to go on-shed as soon as the passenger train is clear.

R.C. Riley

Similar to the 61xx class were the 51xx series 'Prarie' tanks. No. 5167 from the Banbury shed arriving at Oxford with a stopping passenger service in July 1961. Interestingly, the engine is displaying Class 'A' or express train headcode – one lamp over each buffer, wishful thinking perhaps on the part of the crew.

P.J. Kelley

Another clean Worcester engine 7005 *Sir Edward Elgar* approaching the station with an express for Paddington. The engines home shed a coincidence bearing in mind the name it carries.

R.C. Riley

36

Despite attempts at a corporate livery for most engines from 1948, certain exceptions occurred. One of these was the painting of a number of mixed traffic locomotives in lined black. The effect when clean was delightful, 6362 showing this to the full as she heads south on 26.4.56 with an express freight. The neat and tidy youthful enthusiasts are worthy of a second glance.

R.C. Riley

Southern and Western engines side by side, 30861 *Lord Anson* and 6937 *Conyngham Hall* alongside the 'north signal box in February 1954. The various wooden bracket signals were later replaced by the gantry seen in the next picture.

R.C. Riley

Twenty-five years later on a frosty November morning, English Electric type 4, D327 waits at the north end of Oxford station. At this period, 1967, few enthusiasts had time for diesels of almost any sort, yet with the passage of years memories were mellowed and the Class '40's developed a cult following until their withdrawal comparatively recently.

Anthony Vickers

With just a few months to go before the end of steam working those engines that remained presented a sorry sight. Indeed it was often difficult to tell serviceable machines from recent withdrawals. Included in this melancholy scene are Nos 6932, 6983 and 6849 all of them shawn of nameplates.

Roger Sherlock

The western shed at Oxford was constructed primarily of timber and consequently it was a wonder it never caught fire – even so there were several near misses! Caught amidst alternating patterns of light and shade 6947, formerly *Helmingham Hall* stands back to back with a Prarie tank on 29.3.65. The chalked front numberplate a replacement for the cast version which had probably been 'lost'. The bucket above the front buffer was not a standard feature!

Roger Sherlock

6145 on-shed, 31.7.65. Given a choice many drivers would prefer a diesel turn to one with steam, the manual labour and primitive conditions associated with the steam engine were not helped by the general run down condition during the last years. At the time the Oxford shed played host to both steam and diesel traction one of the new 'Brush Type 4' diesels shown behind. Of interest also is the practise of picking out certain parts of the engine in white paint. This was a custom used in many places and helped to brighten up their otherwise shabby appearance. Unfortunately, the white did not stay white for long and the ideal solution would have been to clean the engines properly. But there was neither the labour nor the money available and 6145 along with her many sisters presented an ever more sorry sight until finally withdrawn.

E. Wilmshurst

No western shed was complete without its allocation of pannier tanks. These engines were used for a variety of tasks from shunting to trip working. 57xx series No. 3751 was one of a number, (according to the period this varied from 8 to 10) allocated to Oxford, and is seen refilling its tanks from a rather leaky water column alongside the main line in the summer of 1965.

Roger Sherlock

As the steam locomotive and its facilities became ever more rundown this was reflected both in the appearance of the engines and the general condition of the depôt. 6819 formerly *Highnam Grange* bereft of both name and numberplates alongside the coaling stage where weeds and broken glass abound.

Roger Sherlock

Some of the line of withdrawn engines at Oxford early in 1966 and as seen from the coaling stage. At the time Oxford was host to no less than 27 'Halls' all awaiting their final journey to the scrapyard.

John Fairman

Old and new motive power, with 6145 and it is thought 3677 alongside the coaling stage. In the background is a three car diesel unit painted in the first style of green livery. The diesel sets having replaced the 61xx series of tank engines on suburban workings in the Oxford area.

Roger Sherlock

To conclude the sequence on the Oxford shed what could be more appropriate than one of the impressive BR Class 9's. During the last years the 9F's were responsible for many of the various heavy freights in the area. The design of these engines envisaged ease of access for maintainance, the injectors for example were underneath the cab where a fitter could get to them easily. According to one man, however, this was easier said than done and a Class 9 requiring attention was shunned whenever possible.

Roger Sherlock

Just about to pass Oxford station, 38xx No.3828 takes the down through line at North Junction with a freight for Didcot.

P.J. Cupper

Seen from across the loco yard and down running lines, 7922 *Salford Hall* approaches the station with the York–Bournemouth through train on 23.8.65.

Roger Sherlock

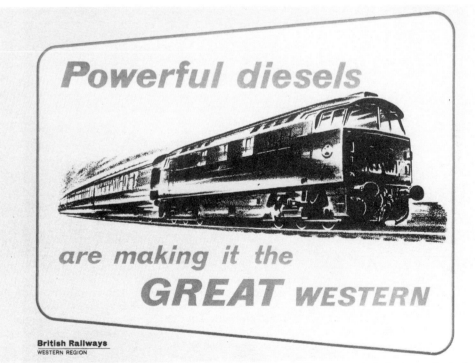

Powerful diesels are making it the GREAT WESTERN

British Railways
WESTERN REGION

In an apparently stubborn fashion, Swindon refused to follow accepted design criteria for its dieselisation programme. Instead adopting a hydraulic transmission pattern compared with the standard electric transmission. In an artists impression of the new 'Western' class the publicity department have had a free reign over the class name. One wonders if the man in charge was perhaps a former GWR man!

British Railways

Unique at Oxford was this upper quadrant signal. All other signals on the Western pointing downwards when at clear. This particular signal was installed in 1949 following instructions from the new British Railways regime that the WR would conform with otherwise standard practice. Accordingly in 1949 a WR circular was issued pointing out that the installation was experimental and that a further report would be produced after evaluation. This further report was a long time coming, for the signal remained in use until 1973 when it was taken down and presented to the National Railway Museum outside which it can now be seen! At the same time the WR issued the follow up circular which pointed out that, '. . .no significant advantages had been found and that subsequent replacement mechanical signalling would follow existing practice'. The GWR and its lower quadrant signals were thus vindicated 25 years after the Western had ceased to exist as a separate company.

British Railways

The politics of railways in the 19th century had resulted in two separate lines to Oxford from the north. The former LNWR route on the extreme left with the GWR lines to the right. The LNWR also had their own station at Oxford, known as Rewley Road, but this closed to passengers in 1951 after which all trains used the WR station. A connection between the running lines of the two routes was established at Oxford North Junction and this can just be discerned from left to right. The LNWR, later LMS and then BR-M line was used by a variety of LMS design engines to reach Oxford although here a BR Standard Class 5 is at the head of an engineers train heading towards Bedford and Bletchley.

R.H.G. Simpson

Past an otherwise deserted railway landscape, LMS 8F 48650 coasts south towards Oxford with a coal train from the midlands. The Bedford lines are visible on the right.

Rodney Lissenden

A 61xx in the role for which it was intended, even if the train consists of just two coaches. No 6129 north of Oxford with a Banbury stopper in the summer of 1963.

Rodney Lissenden

Leaving a smoke screen which was hardly likely to please the allotment holders on the left, 45379 heads underneath Aristotle Lane footbridge towards its home depôt of Bletchley with empty mineral wagons from Oxford via the LNWR line.

Rodney Lissenden

The 841 strong class of LMS Black 5's were common visitors to Oxford. Equally at home on a variety of duties and the equivalent in power to a Western 'Hall'. Unlike the Western machine, however, few were named, 44663 depicted between Wolvercot and Oxford with a mixed freight from the north.

Rodney Lissenden

Another LMS visitor, 44463 heads north towards Wolvercot Junction in June 1963.

Rodney Lissenden

Wolvercot Junction three miles north of Oxford was the divergence of the Banbury and Worcester lines. 6924 *Grantley Hall* coming off the Banbury route with the Bradford–Poole service on 20.6.64. The two bracket signals date from different periods and are to quite separate designs – that on the right being the older.

Rodney Lissenden

Controlling the junction was a brick signalbox on the west side of the line. 6968 *Penrhos Grange* from the Oxford shed crossing over to the Worcester line with a stopping passenger train made up of two Hawksworth bow-roofed coaches.

Rodney Lissenden

Four miles north of Wolvercot at Bletchington on the Banbury line was an extensive cement works. A rail link was provided into the complex which generated considerable rail bourne traffic. On 20.6.64 though there were just four wagons to be moved, a clean 61xx No. 6136 at the head of the train heading south at Wolvercot.

Rodney Lissenden

A final view of Wolvercot Junction as 6999 *Capel Dewi Hall* accelerates on the slightly favourable down grade bound for Banbury with a train of BR Mark 1 stock. In the background the bridge carries the A34 Oxford by-pass around the city whilst the pile of rails is perhaps an indication that some relaying has taken place.

Rodney Lissenden

The Collett 22xx engines were intended primarily for light branch and secondary routes, a far cry from the heavy freight portrayed here. Possibly, 2221 is substituting for a failure as it struggles south near Heyford in 1951.

National Railway Museum, J.F. Russell Smith

Passing the diminutive Fritwell & Somerton signal box, the driver of 34045 *Ottery St. Mary* attacks the gradient bound for the midlands with a football special from Southampton.

R.C. Riley

With the fireman taking a breather, 1008 *County of Cardigan* passes Heyford's down distant signal with a train from Paddington.

National Railway Museum, J.F. Russell Smith

On 27.4.63 Southampton played Manchester United in the semi-final of the F.A. Cup. The neutral ground of Aston Villa in Birmingham was chosen for the match. To cater for the Southampton fans no less than 14 special trains were run from Southampton, whilst a further train commenced at Brockenhurst and travelled via the Somerset and Dorset route. In charge of one of the outward services is 34088 *213 Squadron* passing through Aynho station.

R.C. Riley

Fortunately in 1963 the Southern Region still had the majority of its 140 'Pacifics' in servicable condition and so a number of extra trains would not cause the difficulties that occurred in later years due to a shortage of motive power. 34040 *Crewkerne* at the head of another of the special trains passing Aynho en route for Birmingham.

R.C. Riley

More appropriate to Aynho is No. 4105 at the head of a up stopper on 20.4.63. The station dates from the beginnings of the railways with the continuation of the canopy around the sides of the buildings a feature of the early days. In addition the wider than usual gap between the running rails dates from the broad gauge period. In the background the flyover carries the Banbury direct line on its route towards Princes Risborough and London. Seven months later 4105 was destroyed in a spectacular derailment at Bicester at the head of a coal train.

P.J. Cupper

On the up loop line at Aynho 27.4.63, a much travel stained 28xx, No. 2852 heads south with a loaded mineral train. Much publicity is given nowadays to trains with a gross weight of 1,000 tons or more, although what perhaps is forgotten is that these engines were hauling such loads almost from the time of their introduction by the GWR in 1903.

R.C. Riley

Evidently the Western Region were short of engines to turn out 5307 for a Class 'A' passenger service. A mixed selection of BR and Southern coaches forming an inter-regional train near Aynho in the early 1950's.

National Railway Museum, J.F. Russell Smith

With Aynho Junction in the background, WD 2–8–0 No. 90365 heads north towards Banbury with an empty mineral train on 29.8.62. The engine was one of 730 machines of this type in use on BR during 1962, yet such was the speed of withdrawals that four years later only 140 were left and none survived to be preserved. The engine comes from Woodford Halse on the former GCR line and will probably take the GCR line at Banbury junction bound for the Midlands coal fields.

M. Mensing

Travelling over clean ballast near Aynho, evidence of recent relaying, 6987 *Shervington Hall* is at the head of an up empty van train on 29.8.62. 6987 at the time allocated to Wolverhampton shed.

M. Mensing

Between Aynho Junction and Kings Sutton a set of water troughs laid between the rails allowed engines to pick up water without stopping. 73001 leaves a fine spray beneath its train as it heads north with a featherweight load.

Collection of P. T. Earl

Like the slightly larger 'Hall' class, the 80 'Grange' class engines were equally at home on a variety of duties and suitable for all but the heaviest or fastest trains. Accordingly they were a favourite with many of the crews. 6854 *Roundhill Grange* near King's Sutton with a southbound freight in the early 1950's.

National Railway Museum, J.F. Russell Smith

Originally a member of the 'Star' class, No. 4000 *North Star* was later rebuilt as a member of the 'Castle' class. She is shown here in this later condition at speed near King's Sutton with a London bound train. On the left the distant signal has what is referred to as co-acting arms. The higher one able to be seen from a greater distance whilst as the train approached the lower would be the most visible. Just in front of the signal is a wooden fogmans hut, a reminder of the times when a member of staff had to be present with detonators at each distant signal during periods of thick fog.

National Railway Museum, J.F. Russell Smith

The later series 57xx pannier tanks could be recognised by the large square windows to the front and rear of the cab. Swindon allocated No. 8783 a long way from home as it slowly makes its way south near King's Sutton at the head of a 30 wagon train during 1959.

Collection of P. T. Earl

King's Sutton was also the junction for the secondary route through Kingham to Cheltenham – see later, although here 5930 *Hannington Hall* is shown on the main line with a fast service during the last days of steam working.

Collection of P. T. Earl

At the head of a mixed train of Midland stock 6831 *Bearley Grange* runs non-stop through King's Sutton with an up express. To the right the dereliction within the yard is a sad feature of the last days whilst the pristine condition of the Austin A40 and Sunbeam cars are likely to revive a few memories.

Collection of P. T. Earl

Like Oxford, Banbury (GWR) station was in very poor condition by the time BR took over. The rebuilding of 1939 postponed and in the event only completed during the 1950's. This was the approach to the old station on the 'Up' or London bound side and complete with a suitably dated Co-op delivery van and Morris Minor.

R.C. Riley

Inside the station the gloom of the old building seemed to penetrate everywhere. A group of passengers apparently unaware that the building was mainly held up with steel braces and brick pillar supports! Perpetuating the gloom was the wooden overall roof although this was removed in 1953, three years before the full rebuilding, as it was in imminent danger of collapse. The finger post just visible is a particularly pleasing feature and reads, 'Fast trains to Oxford, Swindon, Westbury & Weymouth'.

British Railways

The rebuilt Banbury was totally different to the past and although a vast improvement from the passenger viewpoint hardly seemed to suit the steam age. Perhaps this was because of the liberal use of concrete and glass. This view taken from the vantage point of the road overbridge on 6.8.60 shows the station at a particularly busy time. 6934 *Beachamwell Hall* leaving the down main platform with the 3.40 p.m. Portsmouth–Wolverhampton service whilst in the bay 6931 *Aldborough Hall* waits with what will later be a stopping service to Leamington. In the yard on the left is another 'Hall' whilst waiting in the platform the diesel unit will form the 7.05 p.m. service to Reading.

M. Mensing

An unidentified 'Castle' at the head of an express from Wolverhampton passing through the new Banbury station. The reporting number, in this case '806' is useful in identifying the type of train. Figures commencing with the digit '8' indicating a Wolverhampton service.

Collection of P. T. Earl

Somehow a 14xx tank and single coach appear a bit lost against the long platforms. No. 1473 at the head of the 5.00 p.m. stopping service to Princes Risborough, via Bicester, in late August 1960.

M. Mensing

Stopping trains from Oxford were invariably the province of the big tanks, 4125 just arrived at Oxford with the 1.08 p.m. service.

M. Mensing

Due to the existence of a second station at Banbury the western station was referred to as 'General' and was also the terminal for stopping passenger trains from the GCR line. As with Oxford a variety of engines could often be seen. A comparatively modern LNER design 'L1' tank No. 67789 waiting to leave at the head of the 1.50. p.m. stopper to Woodford Halse on 25.8.60.

M. Mensing

As the run down of steam gathered momentum, a number of former express types were to be found on lesser duties. Ex LMS 'Royal Scot', No. 46157 *The Royal Artilleryman* at Banbury on a freight working. The engine is in lined green livery and remarkably clean external condition.

M. Sumner

Engineering work on the down main line meant wrong line working for 6906 *Chicheley Hall* at the head of a Leamington train in 1958.

R. Carpenter

In the down bay with a stopping GCR line train, 73066 waits to work the 4.25 p.m. stopping service on 31.5.60.

M. Mensing

Tender first working was unusual over any distance and so it is likely that 48375 would only be going as far as Oxford as it leaves the yard heading south on 26.8.66.

C. Elsey

Just passing under the road bridge at the north end of Banbury station, 92228 receives a 'caution' aspect at the head of a heavy iron ore train. At the top of the tender the open lid of the water filler is perhaps an indication of someone's laziness, the steam spray emitting from under the cab meaning the injector has been turned on.

C. Elsey

With a group of enthusiasts watching from outside the locomotive shed, a dirty 6011 *King James I* leans to the curve approaching Banbury with an express from Paddington.

Collections of P.T. Earl

Following changes in the regional boundaries Banbury came under the control of the Midland Region for the last years of steam, and meaning a number of ex LMS steam designs were based at the shed. In this view 46522 heads a line of LMS types including 44865 and 45289 whilst in the background is an eastern region visitor, B1 61306.

E. Wilmshurst

The last active 22xx, No. 2210 in store outside Banbury shed on 17.7.65. At one time four of these engines were allocated to the depôt, their duties including working the cross country route from King's Sutton to Cheltenham. With the closure of this and other lines the class were redundant and 2210's last journey was to the scrapyard for breaking up.

Courtney Haydon

A study of 5990 *Dorford Hall* in the yards at Banbury in July 1963. Behind the engine is a fine example of a 'cash-register' signal, a variety of indications able to appear according to which route was required. Banbury in 1987 is one of the few places where similar items remain.

Roger Sherlock

Leaving a smoke screen under the Northampton Road bridge, the last active 'Castle' 7029 *Clun Castle* makes a spirited get away from Banbury with a Talylynn Railway special train in late 1965.

J.R. Fairman

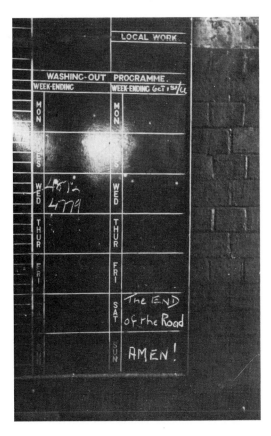

LOCAL WORK

WASHING-OUT PROGRAMME.
WEEK-ENDING   WEEK-ENDING Oct 1st/66

M O N   M O N
E S   S
W E D 4779   W E D
T H U R   T H U R
F R I   F R I
               S A T   The END of the Road
               S U N   AMEN!

Banbury shed closed from 3.10.66, the duty board within the depôt recording the event in suitable form.

J.R. Fairman

All that remains of an unknown 'Hall' at Banbury after the scrap merchants have been at work. Some engines were cut up at the shed simply due to the number of engines withdrawn at the same time meant the scrapyards were just full up.

E. Wilmshurst

71

Included inside the hump cabin was a 10 lever mechanical frame, the levers with short handles indicating an electrically operated mechanism and so needing little effort to move the lever. On the window sill behind are two signal repeaters with lever collars above, whilst standing vertically on the floor is a good old fashioned loud hailer. Ideal for bawling instructions to an engine crew several yards distant.

Collection of Adrian Vaughan

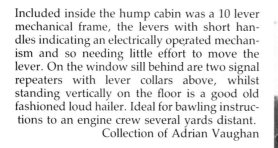

During the years the railways had a monopoly of freight considerable numbers of marshalling yards were established to deal with this traffic. Banbury hump yard opened in 1931 and dealt with many of the wagons interchanged with the LNER Great Central route. The principle of a hump yard was very simple and involved a physical hump over which wagons would be pushed before rolling under their own momentum into the required sidings. Here the hump and its associated ground frame are shown to advantage, the diesel shunter a replacement for steam as early as 1954.

Collection of Adrian Vaughan

Moving now to the line from King's Sutton towards Cheltenham, the first station west of King's Sutton was Adderbury. A delightfully rural setting supplemented by the trees ajoining the platform. 54xx pannier tank, No. 5404 at the head of a single auto coach bound for Kingham from Banbury.

R.H.G. Simpson

Similar in appearance to the 57xx series were the smaller 54xx pannier tanks. 5404 of a number built for light passenger work and able to work auto-trains such as the type shown here. The engine is shown at Adderbury attached to trailer No. W83 whilst working a Kingham train.

R.H.G. Simpson

Watched by a member of the permanent way gang, 5313 enters an otherwise deserted Adderbury station with a Banbury bound freight. Passenger traffic on the section of line between Chipping Norton and King's Sutton and so including Adderbury was withdrawn in 1951.

R.C. Riley

Often seen yet rarely recorded were the activities of the permanent way department. Although at Bloxham between Adderbury and Chipping Norton, a number of staff can be seen returning to the station with a trolley load of rails after what was probably a relaying session. The post carrying the 'C' lamp meant the commencement of a temporary speed restriction.

Collection of M. Sumner

Just east of Chipping Norton a tunnel carried the railway under part of the Cotswolds. Bound for Banbury 5391 has just left the tunnel with the daily pick up freight.

R.H.G. Simpson

Lack of passengers was of course the reason for closure of the line east of Chipping Norton, a single coach was unlikely to provide sufficient revenue to cover the operating costs on what was an expensive line to maintain. A few months before closure an unknown pannier tank propels its auto coach into the daylight from Chipping Norton tunnel.

R.H.G. Simpson.

As with the permanent way department photographs of the local pick up goods services are rare. Although, fortunately one days activities at Chipping Norton are well recorded. In the first view 2–6–2T No. 4113 has arrived at the station from Banbury and busies itself in the yard. The shunter just visible in the background leaning on a point lever.

Tony Molyneaux

After placing wagons for the station in their required positions, 4113 collects any vehicles for onward transmission. The brake van on the extreme right the last to be attached at the end of the train.

Tony Molyneaux

Finally with work complete it is time to refill the side tanks before continuing on to Kingham where no doubt further shunting will take place.

Tony Molyneaux

The town of Chipping Norton had for many years a railway much in keeping with its own period appearance. Although regretfully a journey to Oxford involved a change of train at either Kingham or King's Sutton and so was a time consuming affair. With competition then from the 'bus operators few passengers used the railway. A pannier tank in the process of running round its train at an otherwise deserted station.

Collection of Adrian Vaughan

Framed under the main A44 road bridge another pannier tank slowly enters Chipping Norton from the east with a train for Kingham. The water tank on the left painted in GWR light and dark stone livery almost to the end.

Collection of Adrian Vaughan

Seen from the brake van an unidentified 'Mogul' accelerates away from Chipping Norton towards the tunnel bound for Banbury in 1954.

Collection of Adrian Vaughan

Where trains once ran, Chipping Norton now devoid of trains and track, a sobering sight.

M. Sumner

In happier times with a 'Dukedog' in charge of the four coach 'REC South Midlander' special between Kingham and Chipping Norton during the early 1950's. The open countryside so typical of this line is well portrayed here, whilst the coaches in their neat red and cream livery present an appealing sight.

National Railway Museum, J.F. Russell Smith

Taking true geographical limits, the boundary for Oxfordshire on the Banbury–Cheltenham route comes at Kingham. This station was also a junction with the main line from Oxford towards Worcester. A nicely clean 22xx, No. 2202 leaving the station from the up relief line platform with a pick up freight for Oxford probably from the Chipping Norton line.

Collection of Adrian Vaughan

With the route set for Worcester a former R.O.D. 2–8–0 slowly passes through Kingham with a train of open wagons.

Collection of P. T. Earl

Although strictly out of the area I could not resist including two further views of 4113 shunting at Bourton-on-the-Water a little further down the line. This station was on the continuation of the route from Kingham towards Cheltenham. In the first view 4113 is engaged in moving wagons into the decrepit looking goods shed, the structure of which looks as if it may collapse at any moment. On the extreme right is a token set down point with its protective net, whilst the weeds and grass growing between the sleepers are typical of most yards in the last years.

Tony Molyneaux

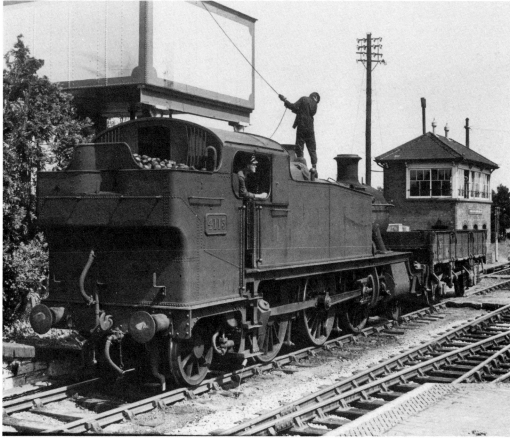

A pause in shunting and time for another fill of the tanks alongside the platform and signal box.
The indented section at the top of the coal bunker was to allow a lamp to be attached as required.

Tony Molyneaux

Just north of Banbury was an extensive private railway system built by the Oxfordshire Ironstone Company. A standard gauge line leading away from some interchange sidings to the actual workings five miles from the main line. Until the mid 'sixties a number of small steam engines were in almost total control of the workings, 'Peckett' 0–6–0ST No. *Sir Charles* at the head of a train of iron ore wagons seen approaching the Friars Hill crushing plant.

Eric Best

The last steam engine was purchased by the firm as recently as 1958. Another 0–6–0ST but this time to the design of the Hunslet company of Leeds. At the quarry it was given the name *Frank* and is shown here shunting a rake of wagons on 26.1.65.

Eric Best

There was also a single sentinal engine at work for some years. Given the name *Phyllis* it dated from 1956 and was finally scrapped only nine years later in September 1965. For some time before this however it had been out of service and is shown here in store during January 1965.

Eric Best

The LNWR station at Banbury was known as Merton Street and situated at the end of the line from Towcester and Verney Junction. Originally with an overall roof, the ravages of time have taken their toll, so that when this view was taken in late December 1959 most of the covering had been removed leaving the remaining wooden platform exposed to the elements. Derby built railcar M79900 waiting to depart with the 3.45 p.m. service to Buckingham. The station finally closed in January 1961.

David Fereday Glenn

Until electrification of the Euston–Birmingham line in 1963 the Western Region competed with its own Birmingham route through High Wycombe, Princes Risborough and Banbury. 'King' class engines were used on the 2 hour expresses right up to their withdrawal at the end of 1962. 6005 *King George II* at the head of the 5.10 p.m. Paddington to Wolverhampton train on Aynho troughs, 29.8.62.

M. Mensing

The Banbury direct line, as it was referred to, joined the line from Oxford at Aynho Junction. A flyover was provided so as to reduce to a minimum delays to trains on either line. Coming off the direct line heading north 4176 is at the head of an iron-ore train from Ardley bound for Banbury in 1962.

M. Mensing.

Following electrification of the former LNW line from Euston the Princes Risborough route was reduced to secondary status narrowly escaping complete closure. In happier times another 'King', this time No. 6022 *King Edward III* heads south from Aynho Junction near Aynho Park Platform with an up express in August 1956.

W. Gilburt

A 'King' in full flight. 6027 *King Richard I* passing Bicester at speed with a Paddington bound train in August 1960.

M. Mensing

In addition to the express services between Paddington and Birmingham there were a number of semi-fasts. 4907 *Broughton Hall* waiting at Bicester (North) with the 4.34 p.m. Paddington–Wolverhampton on 31.5.60. Many of the stations on the direct line were provided with through lines for the fast services, these visible to the left of the engine. This particular working involved waiting for a slip-coach to be dropped off the 5.10. p.m. Wolverhampton express which was then taken forward by the semi-fast service.

M. Mensing

Slip coach working had been a feature of the Western for many years, Bicester being the last place it was practised. Here a converted Hawksworth coach runs under its own momentum on the down through line and about to be brought to a stand by the slip coach guard. On the left is the tail end of the waiting 4.34 p.m. stopping service to Wolverhampton.

M. Mensing

After the coach was safely brought to a stand at the stop signal, the engine from the semi-fast ran onto the main line and pulled the coach forward before setting back with it onto its waiting train. 4907 in the process of drawing forward before setting back onto the front of its waiting train. The special slip coach lamp code shows up well at the rear of the vehicle.

M. Mensing

South of Bicester on the direct line, Blackthorn station had closed in June 1953 and four years later was devoid of platforms although the buildings still remain. On a clear spring morning in April 1957, 5087 *Tintern Abbey* rushes past the deserted site with the 12.10 p.m. Paddington–Wolverhampton express.

R.C. Riley

Princes Risborough in Buckinghamshire is relevant in as much as it was the junction for two branch lines heading back into Oxfordshire. The shorter of the two was the eight and a half mile Watlington branch worked in its last years by a variety of 57xx and 14xx tanks. Here one of the last series of 57xx pannier tanks No. 9657 heads the single coach branch service near Bledlow Bridge Halt in the early 1950's. The engine still in GWR livery.

National Railway Museum, J.F. Russell Smith

Following two minor halts, Chinnor was the first station proper on the branch to Watlington. The addition of a large cement works meaning the rural atmosphere of the site was completely lost. The industrial complex did however generate considerable traffic and so after other goods services were withdrawn in 1961 the railway remained at Chinnor.

Lens of Sutton

Had the intentions of the original promoters been fulfilled then the little branch would have continued to Wallingford, linking up there with the branch from Cholsey. A variety of reasons prevented this and instead the Watlington terminus was sited about ¼ mile from the village of the same name and hardly in an ideal position to serve it. Accordingly, it was an early casualty to competition from the road, this June 1952 view showing 5715 entering the terminus and a travelling railway safe visible on the platform. Booking office receipts from the various stations were sent via the guards van to the branch terminus after which they were placed in the safe and forwarded to Princes Risborough.

R.C. Riley

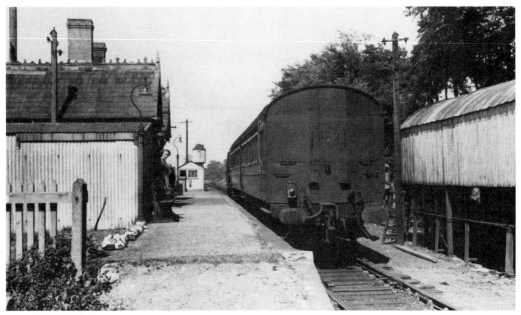

Auto working, meaning the train could be driven from either end was only possible with a suitably equipped engine. Non-auto engines making it necessary to run-round the train at each end of the journey. Awaiting departure from Watlington as a normal service this was the scene on 21.5.56, the lack of many passengers an obvious feature. To the right is the carriage shed, a primitive structure constructed primarily from corrugated iron on a timber framework.

Collection of Adrian Vaughan

Last rites at Chinnor on 29.6.57 and a number of well wishers turned out to witness the final day of passenger services in charge of 57xx No. 4615.

E. Wilmshurst

With the line now open only for freight it was natural it would attract a number of enthusiasts specials. One was on 3.4.60 when green liveried 0–4–2T No. 1473 was in charge of a working from Princes Risborough. The engine is seen detached from its coaches and taking water at Watlington prior to the return trip.

David Fereday Glenn

During the freight only period a number of ex-LMS locos were used on the branch workings, Ivatt 2–6–2T No. 41270 involved in shunting prior to the return to Princes Risborough.

R.H.G. Simpson

During the time the branch was open to passenger traffic, Wallingford was in Berkshire, although as with Didcot, a revision of county boundaries has meant a change of administrative control. Today the station site has been obliterated: however, a little distance away a local preservation society are attempting to re-establish a link with the main line at Cholsey. Similar to Watlington was the use of a single auto coach for many of the passenger services, 14xx. No. 1447 waiting to return to Cholsey with the branch train on 14.5.51.

R.C. Riley

Leaving Princes Risborough the lines to Oxford and Watlington ran side by side for a short distance. 61xx, No. 6152 taking the Oxford route with a seven coach train in the autumn of 1952.

National Railway Museum, J.F. Russell Smith

Last steam engine built for BR was 92220 *Evening Star* which entered service from Swindon in March 1960. Although to a design intended principally for heavy freight work engines of the class were very successful on passenger trains sometimes reaching speeds of 90 m.p.h. Being the last of her type *Evening Star* was always a popular engine on special workings. Perhaps the earliest the LCGB 'Six Counties Special' of 3.4.60 which included a trip over the Thame branch to Oxford. 92220 passing Bledlow at the head of the special train.

David Fereday Glenn

The line from Oxford through Thame to Princes Risborough could accept any engine except members of the 'King' class and was then a useful diversionary route for trains between Oxford and Paddington. One of these diversions was on 9.9.50, with 5031 *Totnes Castle* passing Bledlow's down distant signal on a Paddington bound express. The distant signal is also of considerable interest as it has a wheel in the finial allowing the lamp to be wound up and down the post as required, this alleviated the need for the lampman to climb to the top of the post.

National Railway Museum, J.F. Russell Smith

Characteristic of the western region were its lower quadrant signals, the unique exception at Oxford depicted earlier. For many years most were of timber, with the exception of a few concrete and lattice signals situated at a number of locations throughout the system. Little is known of the reasons for the use of lattice posts for they were to a design totally unlike anything seen anywhere else. The branch through Thame sprouted several of these signals, one depicted in the previous photograph whilst this example served as a starting signal for the up line at Thame itself.

Collection of P.T. Earl

With evidence of a slight steam leakage from the cylinders, 5031 *Totnes Castle* leaves Thame with a diverted London train in 1952.

National Railway Museum, J.F. Russell Smith

The overall roof at Thame survived for the whole period of passenger services, after which the remaining freight services hardly warranted such a luxury and the structure was demolished. For some time oil trains still arrived at the station from Princes Risborough beyond which a set of stop blocks prevented any further movement towards Oxford. Ironically a few miles further on another set of stop blocks prevented trains from proceeding from the British Leyland sidings at Morris Cowley towards Thame. Compared also with the numerous train sheds that formerly existed on the railway few now remain, the sole Western Region example still in service at Frome in Somerset.

Collection of M. Sumner

Holding just a single wagon, Thame goods shed hardly presents a picture of busy activity, although all may well change with the later arrival of the daily pick up goods train. On the left the grounded brake van body served as an additional store whilst the shed office shows evidence of a recent extension.

S. J. Dickson

Another diversion was on 11.9.60 when because of engineering works on the direct line at Bicester the 2.10 p.m. Paddington–Birkenhead service was routed via the Thame branch. It is seen here passing Wheatley behind 5089 *Westminster Abbey* and will rejoin its proper route at Aynho Junction.

M. Mensing

With the giant Morris Cowley car plant in the background 6934 *Beachamwell Hall* heads another diverted Birkenhead service over the branch in september 1960.

M. Mensing

Footbridge and lamp detail at Thame in 1957.

S.J. Dickson

101

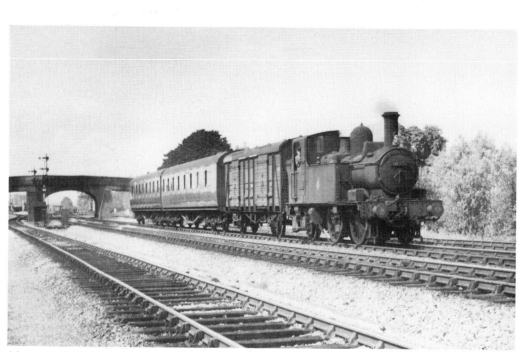

More usual motive power for the Thame branch, 14xx No. 1435 near Hinksey South en route from Oxford towards Kennington Junction with a Thame branch service in August 1959. The van is of Southern Railway origin and used to supplement the limited goods accommodation available within the two coaches.

R.C. Riley

6149 passing Hinksey and near to the end of its 21 mile journey over the Thame branch to Oxford. The train is made up of four coaches with the last an early type of auto-trailer.

R.C. Riley

Leaving Oxford BR Class 4MT tank No. 80039 is at the head of a Bletchley line train of Midland stock on 15.8.59, at the rear of which are two cattle wagons.

R.C. Riley

In 1950, two years after nationalisation locomotive resources at Oxford were concentrated on the former GWR depôt, the Rewley Road shed closed to all traffic and its allocation of engines transferred to the western shed. This particular view was taken in 1954 and shows the structure still standing, if a little delapidated. Demolition did not take place until 1962.

Photomatic

To differentiate between the two stations at Bicester, that on the former LNWR route to Bletchley was designated by BR as London Road. The architecture of the station was very different to any GWR design. Following a revision of boundaries, part of the line came under western control, 61xx tank No. 6106 at the head of a single coach inspection train in the station on 22.10.54.

R.C. Riley

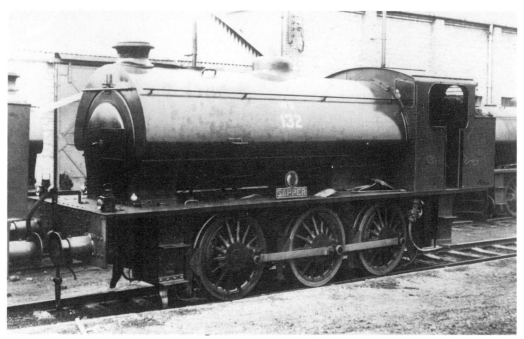

Just outside Bicester London Road was the junction for the extensive Bicester military railway. The military steam system was operated until comparatively recent times by a number of 0–6–0T's to the same type as shown here. No. 132 *Sapper* seen inside the military depôt in March 1960.

R. J. Buckley

The 'Six Counties Limited' special also involved a trip on the Military railway. 92220 *Evening Star* having brought the special train to Oxford where former LNWR 7F No. 49093 took over for the run to Bicester. The train recalled by one present as 'clanking to a stop' at Bicester prior to its run over the military line.

David Fereday Glenn

No. 132 *Sapper* again at the opposite end of the train and about to cross over the main line into the Army sidings, 3.4.60.

David Fereday Glenn

The little branch from Kidlington to Woodstock was another early casualty in BR days and was closed to passengers from 1.3.54. Trains for the branch started from Oxford and if made up of just coaches were usually operated as auto-services. No. 1420 on a Woodstock service at Oxford on 27.2.54.

R.C. Riley

Typical of the branch were its mixed trains and meaning a number of goods wagons were sometimes attached to the rear of any passenger vehicles. Years before, this had been a common feature on a number of lines but opposition from the Board of Trade, allied to an increase in train speeds meant passenger and goods trains had become seperated in more recent times. On the Woodstock branch though the tradition was maintained right to the end, a 14xx tank at the head of a single coach and four wagons near Kidlington in early 1954.

Collection of Adrian Vaughan

106

Specially designated for use over the branch was brake van W68776. The practice of allocating vehicles to specific duties is a feature of railway history now almost totally forgotten.

R.C. Riley

With just a single coach in tow, 5413 approaches the terminus at Blenheim and Woodstock from Kidlington. The overgrown track an indication that closure is not far away.

Lens of Sutton

Waiting at the terminus, perhaps in the hope of attracting some passengers. Small pannier No. 5413 simmers quietly whilst the driver enjoys a well earned rest. With the popularity of nearby Blenheim Palace as a tourist attraction in recent years it is a pity the branch did not survive a few years longer. The railway would be able to compete reasonably well with the 'bus service to Oxford on the nearby A34.

R.H.G. Simpson

Devoid of all evidence of ownership 1420 stands at the terminus after arrival from Oxford. The platform nearest the camera was at one time used for the loading of milk and private horse drawn carriages although it had been out of use for some time when the photograph was taken.

Collection of Adrian Vaughan

R.C. Riley

Last train on the Woodstock branch, 1420 attached to a suitably bedecked auto trailer waiting to return to Oxford on 27.2.54.

ADDITIONAL SUNDAY TRAIN

TO OXFORD, WORCESTER AND GREAT MALVERN

Commencing 27th September, 1953, an additional service will be provided on SUNDAY EVENINGS from London (Paddington) to Worcester and Great Malvern as shown below :—

			p.m.
PADDINGTON	—	— dep	11 . 25
			a.m. (Mon.)
READING GENERAL	—	„	12 . 10
OXFORD	—	— arr	12 . 48
MORETON-IN-MARSH	—	„	1N25
HONEYBOURNE	—	— „	1N40
EVESHAM	—	— „	1N50
PERSHORE	—	— „	2N 0
WORCESTER (Shrub Hill)	—	„	2 . 15
GREAT MALVERN —	—	„	2 . 38

N—Calls to set down only

As with the Banbury direct line the Worcester route from Oxford is but a shadow of its former self, singled in places but fortunately still with a number of fast trains, principally during the morning and evening peaks. Today much publicity surrounds the introduction of an additional train service, the same as it did in 1953 when underneath a reasonable artists' impression of a 'King' class engine a poster was prepared advertising a new train.

British Railways

Coming off the Worcester line at Wolvercot Junction bound for Oxford, BR. Class 4, No. 75008 heads south with a freight from Kingham.

Rodney Lissenden

On 16.5.64, 'Castle' 5054 *Earl of Ducie* was photographed near Yarnton with an Oxford University Railway Society tour. This was one of the engines involved in the celebration of *City of Truro's* record run the previous week, 5054 being worked up to 95 m.p.h., not quite the 100 m.p.h. of *City of Truro* 60 years earlier. The engine is in perfect mechanical order and spotless condition, a credit to the staff of Worcester shed. She was withdrawn for scrap five months later.

Rodney Lissenden

111

'Castle' class engines monopolised the Worcester line services almost up to the cessesion of steam working. Their replacements were the 'Hymek' diesels and later Brush type '4's. Seen from the rear of the train one of the latter engines, Brush Type '4' D1748 leans to the curve approaching Wolvercot Junction with the 7.50 a.m. service from Worcester on 20.5.67.

Anthony Vickers

At Yarnton there were connections with the Fairford branch as well as a direct connection to the Bletchley route. 'Castle' No. 7007 *Great Western* at the head of a Worcester–London train near the actual junction points in 1951.

National Railway Museum, J. F. Russell Smith

At a more leisurely pace a streamlined railcar pauses at Charlbury's down platform with a stopping service from Oxford in 1957.

S. J. Dickson

Charlbury was a timber chalet style station dating back many years and now fortunately the subject of a preservation order. As with Aynho it was originally broad gauge, the available width between the platforms an indication of past times. On what is probably a substitute for a failed diesel turn, a grimy 7926 *Willey Hall* passes through the station on a Worcester express in 1965.

Tony Molyneaux

Kingham in 1964 and the junction for the routes to Banbury and Cheltenham. By this time both lines had lost their passenger service whilst in the background there had once been a bridge carrying the branch avoiding line over the main route. The unusual signal was to assist engine crews in sighting the indication under the station footbridge. Few of this type now remain, although one has been preserved in use at Bewdley North on the Severn Valley line.

Anthony Vickers

Another essential, but rarely photographed item, the gangers inspection trolley. Kingham, 1960.
Anthony Vickers

Western Region disc at Kingham.
British Railways

The steam local of the 1950's. 'Prarie' tank No. 4147 at the head of three coaches on a Worcester–Kingham train nearing its destination. Just visible at the rear of the train is a 'Cordon' or travelling gas tank, examples of which were located at various stations to replenish the tanks of coaches fitted with gas lighting. By this period, however, gas lit coaches were a rarity and so it may be that the wagon was on its way to Swindon for store.

National Railway Museum, P. Ransom Wallis

Passenger services over the Fairford branch lasted until June 1962 after which time freight continued for a further three years. During that period drastic economies were effected in the operation of the route, one of which was the removal of nearly all the signalling. As a form of compensation, marker boards were erected at certain of the sites to inform the engine crews where to stop so the rear of their train would be clear of the various level crossings. One such place was Eynsham, where the '10' wagon board can just be seen in the left distance. 57xx 'Pannier Tank' No. 9654 returning to Oxford with the branch freight shortly before all services were withdrawn.

Tony Molyneaux

The 25 mile Fairford branch commenced its route from Yarnton north of Oxford, although all of its trains started from Oxford itself. In its final years the motive power used on the line was mainly 22xx or 57xx engines. One of the latter type, No. 7404 drawing into Oxford after a trip along the branch with a two coach 'B-set' on 29.9.56.

R.C. Riley

With evidence of recent relaying in the form of sleepers on the opposite platform, 7436 takes water at Witney with a down Fairford train on 14.5.51.

R.C. Riley

The western branch line – unaltered for decades. 7411 entering Witney from Fairford in May 1951 and the signalman waiting to exchange the single line token with the driver.

R.C. Riley

With only a matter of weeks to go before closure 0–6–0PT No. 7404 awaits departure from Alvescot with the 4.26 p.m. Oxford–Fairford local on 19.5.62.

David Fereday Glenn

Of the many features associated with the GWR one of the most familiar must be the corrugated pagodas. Some were used as waiting rooms whilst others, as here, served as lock-ups. Today a few are still to be seen, but not unfortunately this one at Witney. The scene looking towards Fairford in September 1958.

A.E. Bennett

Before the advent of the numerous road bourne parcels carriers the railway had a virtual monopoly of this traffic. A consignment of tea and other groceries being dealt with at Witney in March 1961.

Len Davies

Seen from the platform this was the station building at Alvescot with the entrance to the platform by means of a gate either end of the building. Behind the photographer was a small goods yard, access to which came from a continuation of the station approach road on the right.

A.E. Bennett

Situated amidst an area of open fields Kelmscott & Langford platform was one of several small stopping places opened in an effort to attract additional traffic. 7412 seen awaiting departure for Oxford in July 1958.

E. Wilmshurst

Bustling along the single track in fine style, 7404 approaches Lechlade from Fairford with the 6.10 p.m. local to Oxford. This was the return working for the engine and stock from the 4.26 p.m. down service.

David Fereday Glenn

The terminus of the railway at Fairford and although not strictly Oxfordshire no look at the branch would be complete without including this the last station. As elsewhere the struggles and politics of the early railway were readily apparent to the end, the branch continuing past the station for some distance after which it abruptly terminated in a field some miles short of the intended destination at Cirencester. As a result the goods shed and engine shed were some distance past the station, the roof of the former just visible above the trees in the distance. 57xx tank, No. 7412 about to depart for Oxford in the early 1950's.

National Railway Museum, J.F. Russell Smith

At Lechlade a number of allotments existed opposite the platform, most of these cared for by the railwaymen. One of the regular branch engines, 57xx series pannier tank No. 7411 enters the station with an Oxford train in the summer of 1958.

E. Wilmshurst

Seen from the opposite end of the station, a filthy pannier tank arrives at the terminus from Oxford. Two engines were allocated to the small shed at Fairford, returning to the parent depôt at Oxford from time to time. Of interest is the trackwork in the loading dock on the left, for it is laid with inside-key chairs and meaning the oak keys fitted to hold in the rail in place were on the inside rather than the outside of the line. This practice fell into disuse from about the turn of the century supposedly because of too many accidents to the gangers forced to walk between the tracks when checking the fittings

A. E. Bennett

Complete with bucket and fire irons at the rear of the bunker, 0–6–0PT No. 7404 awaits departure for Oxford with an evening train.

David Fereday Glenn

Venturing south we return again to Radley, junction for the Abingdon branch, 14xx 0–4–2T No. 1425 attached to a single auto coach forming the branch service.

R.H.G. Simpson

As a replacement to steam, a single unit diesel railcar was used. The '2A92' headcode appropriate to the branch service whilst for the benefit of the public a destination blind is also fitted.

R.H.G. Simpson

At Thrupp between Radley and Abingdon an unidentified 57xx pannier and auto-trailer on its way from the terminus towards the junction.

R.H.G. Simpson

A bus service connected with the trains at Radley and is shown here in the station approach. NJO 707 an 'AEC Regal' operated by the Oxford 'bus company.

R.H.G. Simpson

Abingdon station exterior.

R.H.G. Simpson

After the withdrawal of passenger services the branch was retained for the movement of cars from the MG factory. D6353 one of the short-lived Type 2, North British diesels shunting the station with empty carflat wagons.

R.H.G. Simpson

Where else does one attach a canoe? 1420 leaving Abingdon for Radley on an auto-working in
September 1958.

A.E. Bennett

Just into the east side of Oxfordshire was Finmere, part of the former Great Central route from Marylebone to the north. The stations on the former GCR line mostly built with a single island platform and with up and down running lines on either side.

Lens of Sutton

Another line partly in Oxfordshire was the Henley branch from Twyford. The stopping service to Henley formed by a single GWR railcar No. 1 once used on express services between Cardiff and Birmingham.

Lens of Sutton

Today the Henley branch is still open but operated as little more than a long siding. During steam days there were even a number of peak hour services to and from Paddington whilst the famous regatta would also bring considerable extra traffic. In its new guise both the steam trains and mechanical signalling have vanished from the branch and including this unusual bracket outside Henley signal box.

Collection of Adrian Vaughan

The funeral train for Sir Winston Churchill approaching Didcot East on 30.1.65 and appropriately hauled by 34051 *Winston Churchill*. After the state funeral in London the coffin was taken by train from Waterloo to Handborough on the Oxford to Worcester line and the nearest station to Blenheim following closure of the branch from Kidlington.

Les Elsey

To conclude this brief look at the steam era in Oxfordshire what better than a short distance of the main line west of Didcot, this whole area now in the county of Oxfordshire. One of the last series of 'Castles', No. 7032 *Denbigh Castle* bursts under the centre arch of the A34 road bridge at Steventon on its way westwards. Today the 'HST125' sets roar up and down to Bristol and South Wales over the same route and at a much faster rate than 7032 ever did.

David Fereday Glenn

At a decidedly slower pace former WD 2–8–0 No. 90565 draws onto the main line from the loop at Steventon bound for Swindon on 28.12.59. This engine was one of a number of the class allocated to the Western Region, with 90565 hailing from the Gloucester (Barnwood) shed. The station at Steventon was unusual in that passengers wishing to cross from one side to the other had to use the public road bridge, via a path which led up either side of the platform. Steventon station closed in December 1964 and was demolished soon afterwards although the former offices of the GWR on the same site are now occupied as a private dwelling.

David Fereday Glenn

West from Swindon was Wantage Road and like all the stations between Didcot and Swindon now long closed. There was at one time talk of establishing a 'Parkway' facility at the station to serve the numerous villages in the 'Vale of the White Horse' but this came to nothing. One of the Collett modified 2–6–0 'Mogul's running tender first towards Didcot on a misty May morning in 1964.

Les Elsey

Connecting Wantage Road station with the village of the same name was a steam tramway, although this closed to passengers as far back as 1925. For many years afterwards one of the tramways engines *Shannon* was preserved on the platform at Wantage Road although it has since been moved to the preservation depôt at Didcot.

Les Elsey

To the economists of the 1950s and 60s the steam engine was an uneconomic means of operating the railway, whilst likewise the motor car was said to have numerous advantages. At Fairford though in 1969 both forms of transport lie quietly at rest and at the mercy of nature itself.

Philip Kelley